THE RISE OF SKYWALKER

T0066199

ISBN 978-1-5400-8701-0

Visit Hal Leonard Online at
www.halleonard.com

Contact us:
Hal Leonard
7777 West Bluemound Road
Milwaukee, WI 53213

In Europe, contact:
Hal Leonard Europe Limited
42 Wigmore Street
Marylebone, London, W1U 2RN

In Australia, contact:
Hal Leonard Australia Pty. Ltd.
4 Lentara Court
Cheltenham, Victoria, 3192 Australia

STAR WARS: THE RISE OF SKYWALKER

9   FANFARE *AND* PROLOGUE

14   JOURNEY TO EXEGOL

16   THE RISE OF SKYWALKER

22   THE SPEEDER CHASE

25   DESTINY OF A JEDI

28   ANTHEM OF EVIL

30   WE GO TOGETHER

34   THE FINAL SABER DUEL

42   BATTLE OF THE RESISTANCE

37   THE FORCE IS WITH YOU

50   FAREWELL

58   REUNION

55   A NEW HOME

FANFARE AND PROLOGUE

Composed by
JOHN WILLIAMS

Moderately fast

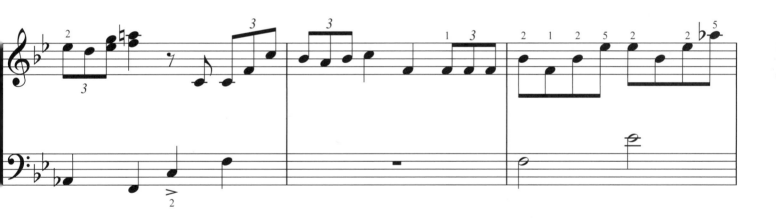

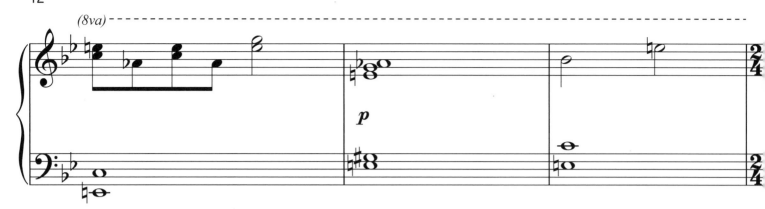

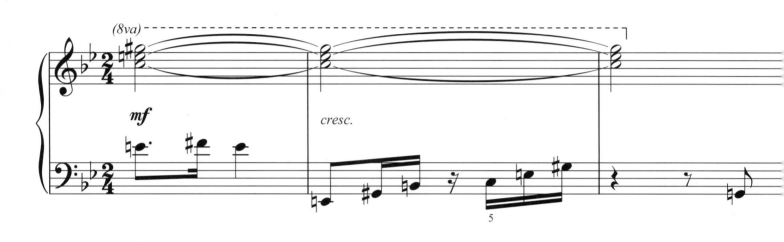

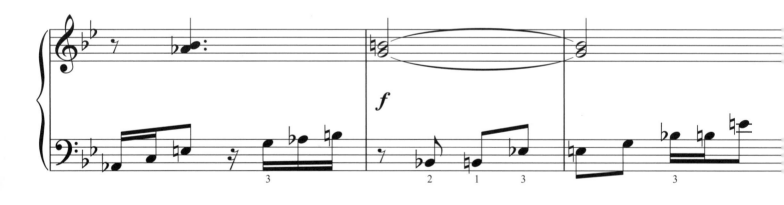

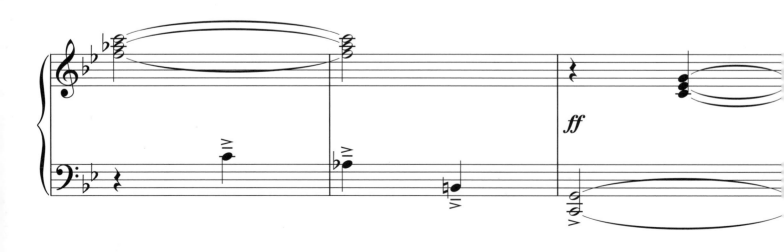

JOURNEY TO EXEGOL

Composed by
JOHN WILLIAMS

Moderately, forcefully

THE RISE OF SKYWALKER

Composed by
JOHN WILLIAMS

Moderately, easily

Slightly faster

Slightly faster

Steadily, faster

rit.

mf

THE SPEEDER CHASE

Composed by
JOHN WILLIAMS

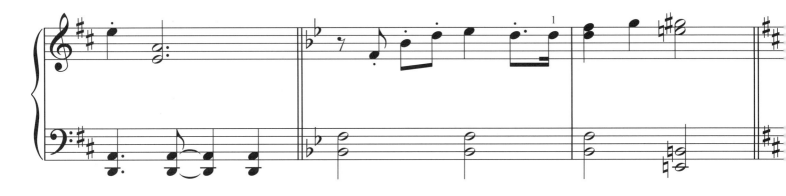

DESTINY OF A JEDI

Composed by
JOHN WILLIAMS

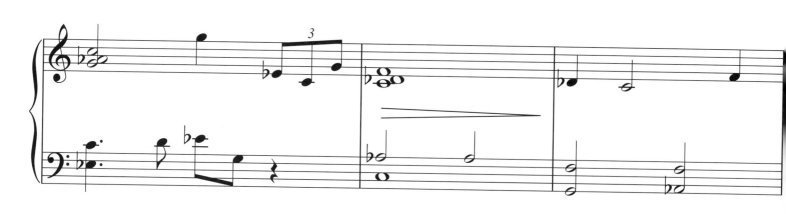

Slowly, expressively

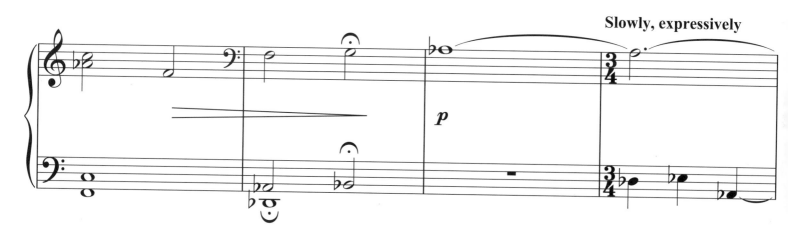

ANTHEM OF EVIL

Composed by
JOHN WILLIAMS

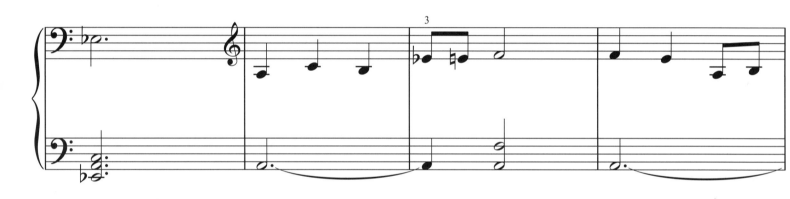

A little slower

Tempo I

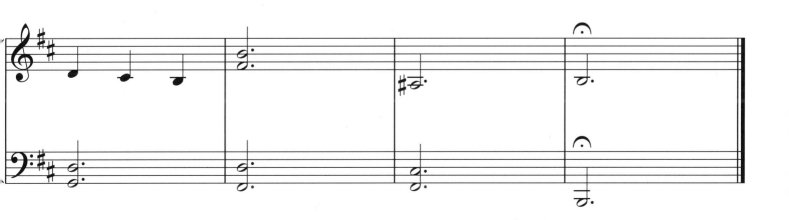

WE GO TOGETHER

Composed by
JOHN WILLIAMS

Moderately slow March

THE FINAL SABER DUEL

Composed by
JOHN WILLIAMS

THE FORCE IS WITH YOU

Composed by
JOHN WILLIAMS

Slowly

BATTLE OF THE RESISTANCE

Composed by
JOHN WILLIAMS

Moderately fast, relentlessly

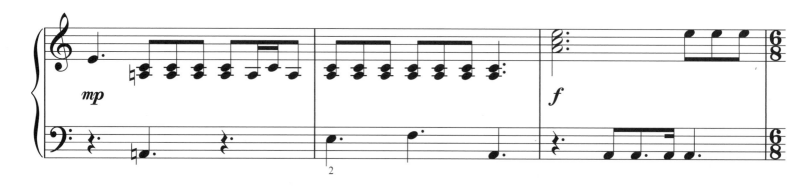

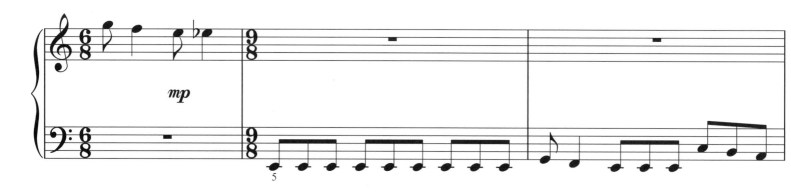

49

FAREWELL

Composed by
JOHN WILLIAMS

52

A little faster

mf

f

Moderately slow

mp *lightly*

A NEW HOME

Composed by
JOHN WILLIAMS

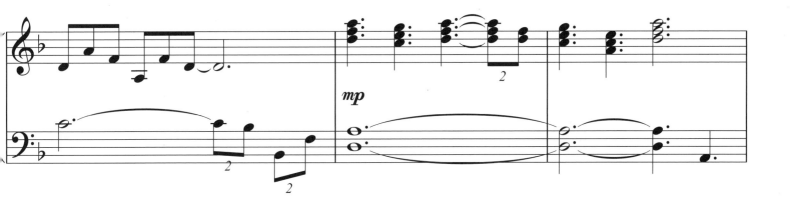

REUNION

Composed by
JOHN WILLIAMS

Fanfare

Moderately fast

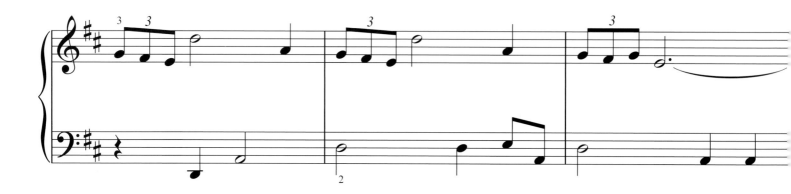

62